MW01411287

# It Tastes Terriffic Anyway

# Kosher It Ain't

# But

# It Tastes Terriffic Anyway

Aaron Cantor

Copyright © 2003 Aaron Cantor
All rights reserved.

All rights, national & international are reserved.
No part of this book may be reproduced by print, audio, video, or any electronic
means without written permission from the author, without exception.

ISBN 1-59109-852-1

Kosher It Ain't

But

It Tastes Terriffic Anyway

# Table of Contents

# Thank You
# To
# Shirley Smoler

This nice lady proof read my manuscript. I tried to type it correctly, but my punctuation leaves a lot to be desired, as English was not my greatest subject in school.

To begin, let me say that I am not a graduate of some fancy-schmancy cooking school, nor am I a chef or a gourmet cook.

My definition of a Gourmet is "a glutton in a tuxedo".

My love of good food and it's preparation began the summer I was six years old and had gone to spend the summer with my maternal grandmother and, no, I will not tell you what year that was, but suffice it to say that Bobbeh had a Monarch cook range, the wood-burning kind, with three lids on the left, the griddle on the right, a hot water tank on the side and a warming oven above. If you can remember the stove I have just described, you must be about as old as I am (gotcha).

I would venture to say that I felt like I had chopped a ton of wood for that stove by the end of the summer (somewhat akin to Tom Sawyer whitewashing the fence). It didn't seem like a lot of fun at the time, but looking back through the eyes of middle aged nostalgia, it was probably the best summer I ever had.

That wonderful lady never owned a cookbook that I ever saw, but with a pinch of this and a dash of that, she could conjure up some of the most wonderful goodies you could possibly imagine.

Having served in the military as a flyer for many years, I have been privileged to visit most of the civilized or semi-civilized countries of the world and have gotten recipes from everywhere, so I have put together a few of my favorites for your enjoyment (the easy to fix ones).

The idea came to me, that it would be good to have some recipes at hand that would let the average person get home with only two hours before company is due to arrive, and still be able to put a nice meal on the table without a lot of time and fuss. There are a few exceptions, but most take under two hours, so press on.

I have included some recipes for making stocks of various

kinds, as food has to have a foundation, (for making soups and sauces).

There is no geographical order to this book, but just for fun, I have included a recipe for Scotland's infamous haggis, (not one of my favorites, Lassie). Once you read the ingredients, you will know where the term "Scotland the Brave" comes from.

A cookbook is only a guide, so for the first time out of the chute, follow the book. After that, any cook worthy of the title is going to get creative, so have at it.

I don't know about you, but my kitchen has a well stocked spice rack, as well as several strings of GARLIC, as cooking without garlic is not cooking—it is only pretending.

I hope you enjoy tasting these as much as I enjoyed putting this book together for you.

BON APETIT

*Dedicated to Sarah Blanche Jarman*

*My Maternal Grandmother*

*(Of blessed memory)*

# Chicken Stock

Everything has to have a foundation, (even food) so we will begin with some recipes for making basic stocks.

5 lbs chicken parts (backs, necks, and wings)
2 large leeks, washed and coarsely chopped
12 peppercorns, lightly crushed
3 cloves garlic, peeled and crushed
1 large stalk celery
1 large onion, halved
2 whole cloves
3 sprigs parsley
3 carrots, coarsely chopped

Put chicken parts in a large pot and add ten cups cold water. Bring slowly to a simmer over moderate heat, skimming as necessary with a slotted spoon to remove any scum that rises to the surface. When it begins to simmer, add the rest of the ingredients. Pierce each onion half with a clove and add to the pot. Return to a simmer. Then, reduce heat to maintain a simmer. Cook 3 hours, uncovered. Cool to room temperature. Strain through clean cheesecloth in a wire strainer. Refrigerate. When ready to use, lift off any congealed fat on surface. Stock may be refrigerated for up to a week, or frozen for a couple of months.

# Fish Stock

5 lbs fish bones and heads, ¼ cup unsalted butter
2 tbsp virgin olive oil, 3 cups coarsely chopped onion
½ cup minced shallot, 2 carrots coarsely chopped
1 cup dry white wine (Reisling is good), 3 sprigs parsley
1 bay leaf, 12 black peppercorns lightly crushed

Place the fish bones and heads in a 1 gallon stock pot. Add cold water to cover and soak for 1 hour. Drain and return bones to dry pot. Add butter and olive oil and cook over moderate heat for 10 minutes, stirring to melt butter and coat the bones. Add onions, shallot, and carrots. Reduce heat to moderately low, and sauté stirring occasionally for 15 minutes. Add wine and cook until wine is almost completely evaporated. Add 10 cups of cold water along with parsley, bay leaf, and peppercorns. Bring to a simmer, skimming as necessary with a slotted spoon to remove any scum rising to the surface. Reduce heat to maintain a simmer and cook 30 minutes. Cool to room temperature. Strain through clean cheesecloth in a wire strainer. Refrigerate. Stock may be refrigerated for up to a week, or frozen for a couple of months.

# Veal Stock

2 lbs veal shanks
2 lbs veal bones
1 large onion, halved
2 whole cloves
3 leeks, coarsely chopped
½ lb carrots, coarsely chopped
3 sprigs parsley
1 tsp thyme
12 black peppercorns, lightly crushed

Preheat oven to 450 degrees F. Place veal shanks and bones in a large roasting pan and bake 45 minutes. Pierce each onion half with a clove. Add onion, carrots and leeks to pan and bake an additional 30 minutes. Transfer bones and veggies to a large stock pot. Add 5 cups of water to the roasting pan and bring to a boil on top of stove, scraping bottom of pan with a wooden spoon to release all deposits, and pour into stock pot. Add 8 cups of cold water, parsley, thyme and peppercorns. Bring slowly to a simmer, skimming as necessary to remove scum from surface. Reduce heat to maintain a simmer and cook for approximately 8 hours. Cool stock to room temperature then strain through clean cheesecloth in a wire strainer, and refrigerate. When ready to use, lift off any congealed fat from surface. Stock can be refrigerated for up to a week, or frozen for a couple of months.

# Vegetable Stock

When you want a light soup base, or you are fixing a meatless meal, a veggie stock is very handy to have around.

8 whole cloves
4 onions, halved
1 bulb of garlic, broken up into unpeeled cloves
4 leeks, washed and coarsely chopped
2 parsnips, unpeeled and coarsely chopped
2 large carrots, unpeeled and coarsely chopped
1 lb tomatoes, quartered
½ lb mushrooms, thickly sliced
1 large bunch scallions, coarsely chopped
4 tbsp virgin olive oil

Pierce each onion half with a clove. Combine all ingredients in a 1—gallon stockpot and stir to coat the vegetables with oil; sauté over moderate heat for ten minutes. Add 12 cups cold water. Bring slowly to a simmer, reduce heat to maintain a simmer and cook 4 hours. Cool to room temperature, strain through clean cheesecloth in a wire strainer and refrigerate. Stock may be refrigerated for up to a week or frozen for a couple of months.

# Aioli Sauce

## Italy

This is garlic mayonnaise. It is a real delight on a salad, and can be used on cold meat slices, or make extra and use it as a veggie dip. Bon Gusto!

6 cloves of garlic
1 large egg
1 cup olive oil
(I like Spanish olive oil, it has a fruitier flavor)
1 tbsp lemon juice

Crush and peel the garlic, and place in blender. Add egg and blend for 15 to 20 seconds. Add oil slowly through the top of the blender creating an emulsion. Stir in the lemon juice by hand with a whisk.

# Basic Tomato Sauce for Pasta

Pretty obvious where this one comes from wouldn't you say? This is the quickie easy to fix version. I will do the 2 day version in another book.

3 tbsp olive oil
2 cups lightly packed parsley
4 small cloves of garlic, minced
½ tsp thyme
¼ tsp ground sage
¼ tsp powdered oregano
2-8 oz. cans tomato sauce
1½ cups veal stock (see page 3)
1 cup water
¼ cup wine (Chianti)
2 small dried red chili peppers, finely chopped
Pinch of salt

In a sauce pan over medium heat, combine olive oil, parsley, garlic, thyme, oregano and sage. Cook, stirring until parsley is soft but still bright green. Stir in tomato sauce, water, wine, veal stock, and chopped chili peppers. Bring to a boil, then reduce heat and simmer gently uncovered for approximately 20 minutes. Salt to taste

Makes 3—4 cups of sauce, which will accommodate approximately 6 servings of pasta

# Cilantro — Lime Salsa

## Mexico

This is a very refreshing salsa that goes well with shrimp, hard boiled eggs, cold veggies, or anything else you like to dip.

1 small onion, very finely chopped
1 heaping cup fresh cilantro, chopped
½ cup parsley, chopped
½ cup olive oil
8 tbsp lime juice
2 tbsp white wine vinegar
2 cloves garlic, well minced
2 small jalapenos, stemmed, seeded, and well minced

Mix all ingredients well in a non-metallic mixing bowl, and place in refrigerator for 1 hour.

Makes 2½ - 3 cups

# Dipping Sauce

## Thailand

6 oz. water
2 oz. soy sauce
2 tbsp peanut oil
4 cloves garlic, peeled and crushed
2 tbsp ginger root, chopped very fine
2 red chilies, seeded and chopped very fine
4 tsp hot paprika

Place ingredients in blender and puree for 1 minute. Pour into a dipping bowl and get ready for a taste treat.

This is great for cold shrimp, all kinds of veggies, or cold meat slices.

# Green Curry Paste

Krung Kaeng Keo Wan

Thailand

1 tbsp dried krachai*
2 good size strips of lime peel, dried and minced
3 tbsp coriander root, chopped fine
6 — 8 serrano chilies, seeds and veins removed
(Leave the seeds and veins in if you like it super hot)
1 stalk lemongrass, minced (obtained at Asian deli)
2 tbsp minced garlic
2 tbsp minced shallot
1 tsp shrimp paste (obtained at Asian deli)
3 tbsp sesame oil

Combine all ingredients in a blender and blend until relatively smooth, adding the oil as necessary to ease the blending process. Store covered in refrigerator until ready for use. This can be used on poultry, seafood or pork.

Makes approximately 1/3 cup

*Krachai, also known as Rhizome is of the ginger family. It can usually be found in Asian delicatessens. It usually comes shredded and in small bags.

# Guacamole

## Mexico

1 large avocado
1 cup cottage cheese
4 tbsp salsa (see page 7)

Put cottage cheese in blender. Blend until smooth. Cut avocado in half and remove seed, peel and place in blender and blend, adding salsa until the whole mixture is smooth. Place in a ceramic serving bowl and refrigerate until ready to serve.

Serves 4—6

# Hummus

### Israel and other points Middle Eastern

2 14 - 16 oz. cans garbanzo beans
½ cup tahini (sesame paste from the gourmet section)
Juice of 1 lemon
3 cloves garlic, peeled and crushed
3 tbsp olive oil
½ cup parsley

Drain 1 can garbanzo beans and place in blender, add second can with juice to the blender. Add tahini, lemon juice, and garlic. Put blender on puree and blend until very smooth. Put mixture on a platter and spritz with olive oil. Garnish with parsley.

In case you haven't figured it out, Clyde, this is a dip or a spread, whichever you prefer.

Serve with raw veggies and Middle Eastern flat bread.

Serves 8 — 10

# Marinara Sauce

## Italy

4 cloves garlic, halved
3 tbsp olive oil
1 large can of tomatoes (approx. 1 lb)
¼ tsp freshly ground pepper
½ tsp basil
½ tsp oregano
Pinch of salt
½ cup chopped parsley
1 lb cooked medium shrimp (Shelled, de-veined
& de-clawed), cut into bite-sized pieces.

In a heavy frying pan sauté the garlic in oil until golden. Drain liquid from tomatoes into the pan, crush the tomatoes, and add to the pan along with the pepper, basil, and oregano. Simmer gently, uncovered for approximately 30 minutes. Raise heat at the end of cooking time to thicken the sauce, if needed. Add the cooked shrimp and the parsley to the sauce just until heated through (approximately 5 minutes).

Can be served over any kind of cooked pasta

Serves 4 — 6

# Nuoc Mam

Vietnamese Spicy Fish Sauce

If you served in Vietnam, this one is no stranger. It is a bit aromatic, to say the least.

2 red chili peppers, finely minced
4 cloves garlic, pressed
3 tsp sugar
½ cup Vietnamese fish sauce (obtained at Asian deli)
2 tbsp lime juice
1 cup water

Mash peppers, garlic, and sugar into a paste. Add fish sauce, lime juice, and water. Place in blender and blend well. Seal in Mason jar and refrigerate until ready to use.

Makes approximately 1 cup (if you want more, double it)

# Pesto Sauce

### A la Genovese

### Italy

This is one of the great sauces of Italy, and very simple to make. It can be used with pasta or over tomatoes, as well as almost any food you want to jazz up a little.

    2 cups packed fresh basil leaves, washed and well
    drained
    1 cup fresh grated Parmesan cheese
    ½ cup virgin olive oil

Place ingredients in blender at high speed until you have a very rough puree. You can add a few pine nuts for variety if you wish.

Makes approximately 1 ½ cups

# Spicy Cocktail Sauce

## New Orleans Style

2 tbsp onion, very finely chopped
2 cloves garlic, very finely chopped
1½ tbsp butter
1 cup water
½ cup tomato paste
1½ tbsp prepared horseradish
2 tsp lemon juice
½ tsp dry mustard
¼ tsp red pepper flakes
Pinch of salt

In a 1—2 qt saucepan, cook the onion and garlic in the butter until tender. Add remaining ingredients and stir well. Bring to a boil, reduce heat and simmer uncovered for approximately 10 minutes, or until it reaches the desired thickness.

It can be served warm or cold and goes particularly well with fried frog legs.

Makes approximately 1 cup

# Spicy Lime Sauce

## Cambodia

This can be used as a dipping sauce or a salad dressing, as it is fairly mild and will not burn your innards to a crisp.

3 cloves garlic, peeled
2 fresh red chilies, stemmed and seeded
¾ cup water
2 tbsp fish sauce (see page 13, or go to Asian deli)
Juice of 1 med lime
3 tbsp sugar

Combine all ingredients except sugar in blender. Blend well then add sugar little by little through top of blender.

Makes 1 full cup

# Tartar Sauce

### Baton Rouge Style

Most recipes from Cajun country are fairly spicy, (come on baby light my fire) but a little spice in your life is good for you so press on.

1 cup mayonnaise (use Aioli sauce from page 5)
¼ cup sweet pickles, chopped very fine
2 ½ tbsp green onions, chopped very fine (scallions, Clyde)
1 tbsp parsley, chopped very fine
1 tbsp lemon juice
A very healthy dash of green Tabasco

Puree all these ingredients in a blender for 1 minute.

This goes well with any seafood (redfish, crawfish, gator tail, shrimp; whatever).

Makes approximately 1 ¼ - 1 ½ cups

# Thai Chili Sauce

The Thai name is Nam Prik

3 tbsp dried shrimp, soaked and drained
5 cloves garlic, peeled
3 red chilies (seeds and veins out for mild, in for hot)
1 tsp sugar
3 tbsp lime juice
3 tbsp fish sauce (see page 13 or go to Asian deli)
¼ - ½ cup of minced raw eggplant

Combine all ingredients in blender and blend to a smooth consistency.

This can be spooned over rice or steamed veggies, or used as a dip.

Makes approximately ½ cup

# Tomato and Caper Sauce

France

2 hard-boiled eggs
1 ½ tbsp shallot, chopped very fine
1 tbsp parsley, chopped very fine
4 tbsp red wine vinegar
¾ cup peeled tomato, chopped very fine
(I don't seed, so why should you?)
1/3 cup olive oil
1 ½ tbsp capers (don't rinse)
Salt and freshly ground pepper to taste

Chop the eggs very fine. Mix with the shallot, parsley, vinegar and tomato in a bowl. Stir in the olive oil. Blend in the capers with a whisk. Serve at room temperature.

This sauce goes quite well with most sliced meats.

Makes 1 ¼ - 1 ½ cups

# Sauce Bordelaise

France

1 cup red wine (try Merlot, my favorite)
1 cup veal stock (see page 3)
¼ cup mushrooms, chopped fine
4 tbsp shallots, chopped fine
1 tbsp butter
2 tbsp parsley, chopped fine
Salt and freshly ground black pepper (to taste)
1 tbsp cornstarch mixed with 2—3 tbsp water
(1 clove of garlic, chopped fine is optional)

In France this sauce is made without garlic.

Mix wine and soup stock in a saucepan and cook till reduced to half. Sauté the shallots and mushrooms in butter until tender; add the wine and stock mixture together with the parsley, salt and pepper, and simmer for a few minutes. Thicken with the cornstarch and water mixture.

This sauce will compliment all meats.

Makes 1 ½ - 1 ¾ cups

# Bechamel Sauce

### Basic White Sauce

This has a French name, but was in fact, invented by the Greeks.

2 cups milk
3 tbsp yellow onion, very finely chopped
1 bay leaf
½ stick of butter
4 tbsp flour
Salt and freshly ground black pepper (to taste)

Bring the milk to a simmer. Add the onion, bay leaf and pepper. Simmer for a few minutes, then strain and return to the stove. Melt the butter and stir in the flour. Remove the milk from the burner and stir in the flour/butter mixture. Continue to simmer, stirring until thick, approximately 10 –12 minutes. Remove and stir in the salt.

This sauce is quite good for any creamed meat dishes, or fish. It is wonderful over baked rabbit or chicken as well.

Makes approximately 2 cups

# Sauce Provencale

### France

4 med tomatoes, peeled, seeded and cut up
½ tsp sugar
¼ cup scallions, chopped very fine
1 clove garlic, minced
6 tbsp butter
½ cup dry white wine
2 tbsp snipped parsley

Sprinkle tomatoes with sugar and set aside. In medium saucepan, cook union and garlic in 2 tbsp of butter until tender, but not browned. Add wine and cook over high heat, stirring occasionally, approximately 3—4 minutes or until the liquor is slightly reduced. Stir in tomatoes, the remaining butter, and the parsley, and heat through. Serve with either beef or pork.

Makes approximately 2—2 ¼ cups

# Avocados with Hazelnut Oil

## France

2 large ripe avocados
8 —10 tsp hazelnut oil
1 large lime, quartered
4 sprigs watercress
2 dozen hazelnuts (filberts to you, Clyde), skins removed.

Halve the avocados lengthwise and remove the pits. Place each half cut side up on individual plates, and spoon 2 tsp of hazelnut oil into each piece. Garnish with a lime wedge and a sprig of watercress.

Spread the filberts on a baking sheet and toast in a 300 degree oven for approximately 10 minutes. When they are cool enough to handle, divide evenly on the 4 plates as an accompaniment.

Serves 4

# Baked Garlic

I found this one everywhere from Montclair to Moscow

Place whole heads of garlic (lots of them) in a baking dish, and bake at 325 degrees for approximately 1 hour. You can then pull off individual cloves and squeeze the garlic which is now a paste, directly onto thinly sliced cocktail ryes (which have been previously brushed with olive oil and toasted).

It makes a delicious hors d'oeuvre, and the garlic when it is cooked takes on a sweet, rather than a pungent flavor.

As I said at the top of the page, you will find this one anywhere that you find garlic growing.

# Baked Mushrooms

## Italy

1 lb med mushrooms (approximately 20)
2 tbsp fresh butter
3 tbsp virgin olive oil
1 large clove garlic, minced
2 tbsp chopped parsley
½ tsp salt
1/8 tsp oregano
1/8 tsp thyme
¼ cup soft bread crumbs
¼ cup grated Romano cheese
Pinch freshly ground black pepper
Pinch freshly ground nutmeg

Remove stems from the mushrooms, reserve the caps. Chop the stems very fine. In medium skillet over medium heat, place the butter and oil. When the butter is melted, add chopped stems and cook stirring until juices have evaporated and stems are lightly browned. Mix in garlic, parsley, salt, pepper, nutmeg, and crumbs. Remove from heat. Mound equal amounts of cooked mixture into caps and sprinkle with Romano cheese. Place on greased baking sheet, and bake in 400 degree oven for approximately 20 minutes.

# Chicken Liver Pate'

France

½ cup butter
1 lb chicken livers
1/3 lb mushrooms, finely chopped
¼ cup parsley, finely chopped
¼ cup scallions, finely chopped
½ tsp salt (use kosher salt—it's only half as salty as iodized).
2 HEALTHY tbsp Brandy
½ cup dry red wine
½ lb butter, cut up into small chunks
1 can black truffles, minced

In large frying pan over medium heat, melt ½ cup butter. Add chicken livers, mushrooms, parsley, scallions, and salt. Cook stirring often, until livers are browned on all sides, but still pink in the center. In a small pan warm brandy and set aflame, pour over livers and shake skillet until flame dies out. Add wine and heat to simmering. Remove and let cool to room temperature. Puree livers and liquid in blender. Add chunks of butter and stir in truffles. Pour mixture into a dipping bowl and refrigerate until it is firm. This will keep in the fridge for about a week.

# Crispy Prawns and Cauliflower

## Thailand

1 small head cauliflower (in florets)
Juice of 1 lemon
2 tbsp soy sauce
1 lb raw shrimp (peeled and de-veined leave claws on)
3 cloves of garlic, peeled and crushed
Peanut oil for deep frying

Cook cauliflower in boiling water until just tender, but still with a little bite. Drain and refresh in cold water. Drain again and place in a large mixing bowl and squeeze half a lemon worth of juice over it. Add 1 tbsp of soy sauce, toss and place in fridge while preparing prawns and batter. Place prawns in a bowl and add remaining half of lemon juice, soy sauce, and crushed garlic. Toss and place in fridge while you make the batter.

For the batter, you will need:
4 oz flour
Pinch of salt
1½ tsp baking powder
8 oz cold water

Sift flour, salt, and baking powder into a bowl. Gradually whisk in enough water to make a smooth batter (no lumps Clyde). Dip prawns and cauliflower florets in batter one at a time, and drain any excess. Deep fry in oil in small batches, until golden and prawns are cooked through. Drain on paper towels and serve with Thai dipping sauce. (See page 8)

Serves 4 – 6

# Fried Squid

## Calamari a la Romana

½ - ¾ lbs small cleaned squid
Flour for dusting
Olive oil for frying (approx. 1" deep in frying pan)
2 large eggs, slightly beaten
Pinch of salt, and a pinch of ground black pepper

Cut the squid into ½" wide rings. Leave the tentacles intact. Dry with paper towels then dust with flour. Heat oil, then coat rings with the beaten egg. Place them one at a time in the hot oil. Cook until they are a light golden color, approximately 2 minutes. Don't overcook, as squid will become tough and rubbery if overcooked. Drain on a paper towel, salt and pepper to taste. Serve immediately, garnish with either lemon or lime wedges.

Serves 6 — 8

# Garlic Eggplant

Bucharest, Romania

1 med to large eggplant
2 med onions, minced
4 cloves garlic, crushed
1 large tomato, chopped
¼ cup virgin olive oil
1 tbsp red wine vinegar
1/8 tsp salt
1 tsp freshly ground black pepper
Black olive slices for garnish

Bake the eggplant whole until tender, turning occasionally to cook evenly, (approximately 25 minutes). Peel off the skin. Put eggplant and all ingredients except the olive slices into a deep bowl and chop very fine. Serve on pumpernickel or rye cocktail slices (toasted) using the olive slices as a top garnish on each.

This is also known as "Poor man's Caviar".

In Sicily, they have a relish called "CAPONATA", which is quite similar. See, folks aren't really very different.

Serves 4 — 6

# Olive Paste and Roquefort

## Rota, Spain

¼ lb pitted black olives
2 med cloves fresh garlic, put through a press
3 tbsp pine nuts
4 tbsp fresh virgin olive oil
½ inch slices long crusty French bread
½ lb Roquefort cheese
Black olive slices for garnish

Place olives, garlic, pine nuts, and olive oil in a blender and puree.

Spread very thinly on bread slices. Cover with Roquefort and garnish with black olive slices.

Try this very tasty treat with a glass of hearty red wine.

Serves 6 — 8

# Piroshki

### Vilna, Lithuania

My Zaideh's (My paternal grandfather) homeland

½ lb ground lamb
2 cloves garlic, chopped fine
1 small onion, chopped fine
4 tbsp olive oil
¾ tsp salt
½ tsp freshly ground black pepper
¼ tsp thyme
½ tsp poppy seeds
1 egg, beaten, for meat mixture
¼ cup soft bread crumbs
Pastry dough (any two crust recipe will do)
1 egg white, to brush rounds before filling
1 egg slightly beaten, to brush tops before baking

Mix the garlic with the ground lamb. Sauté the onion in olive oil, add the meat mixture and season with pepper, thyme, salt, and poppy seeds. Cook over a low flame approximately 15 minutes, stirring occasionally. Cool; work in the egg and bread crumbs. Keep chilled until ready to make the turnovers. Roll pastry dough into a rectangle and cut into approximately 2" circles. Brush each with egg white, and place a tsp of meat mixture on each circle, fold over and seal with the tine of a fork, or a pastry wheel. Prick a hole in each. Brush each with beaten egg. Place on a lightly greased baking sheet, bake in a pre-heated oven at 400 degrees for 15 minutes.
Makes approximately 45—50 turnovers

# Provencal Anchovy Sauce

### France

3 cans (3 oz each) anchovy fillets, drained well and chopped
¼ cup red wine vinegar
¾ cup extra virgin olive oil
½ cup parsley, finely chopped
4 med cloves of garlic
¼ tsp freshly ground black pepper

Combine all ingredients in a blender and puree. Cover overnight.

Use as a dip for raw veggies and/or cold cooked shrimp, or hard boiled egg halves with French bread.

This makes a dandy appetizer, or if you like you can make it the whole meal with a bottle of your favorite wine.

Red or white, it's your choice.

Serves 14—15

# Roman Style Artichoke Platter

### Italy

12 med artichokes (approx 3" diameter)
2 tbsp lemon juice
2 tbsp red wine vinegar
2 tbsp fresh chopped mint leaves
¼ tsp salt
½ tsp oregano
½ tsp grated lemon peel
¼ tsp freshly ground black pepper
¾ cup virgin olive oil

Cut off and discard the top third of each artichoke. Peel off outer layer down to the pale green inner leaves. Peel the green surface from the base of the stem; then trim the stem end. In a 3 quart pan cover the artichokes with boiling salted water and cook covered for about 15 minutes or until they are easily pierced. Drain well and arrange in a shallow serving dish. In a small bowl, combine lemon juice, vinegar, mint, salt, oregano, lemon peel, and pepper. Using a whisk gradually beat in the olive oil until well blended. Pour dressing over artichokes and let stand until dressing is well absorbed. Serve with artichokes standing stem up (Attencione).

Serves 4

# Snails with Herb Butter

## France

1 can (24 count) large cooked snails, drained
¼ lb fresh butter
2 med cloves garlic, minced
2 tsp chives, minced
2 tbsp parsley, minced
8 tbsp Romano cheese, grated
1 loaf French bread, sliced medium thin

Rinse snails in cold water, drain and set aside. Mix butter, garlic, chives, and parsley. Put a dab of the butter mixture and a snail in each of the clean dry snail shells, (ceramic reusable snail shells can be purchased in a specialty or gourmet shop). Seal in the snails with the remaining butter mixture, then press the buttered surface into the Romano cheese.

Arrange the shells in a small baking dish and bake in a 475 degree oven for 6 minutes, or until cheese is slightly browned and the butter is bubbling. Serve with French bread slices.

Serves 4

# Stuffed Clam Appetizer

## Italy

2 dozen hard shell clams (well scrubbed)
2 cups water
¼ cup fresh butter
1 large clove garlic, finely minced
3 tbsp parsley, finely minced
3 tbsp Italian style bread crumbs

Place clams in a large pot with the water; cook over moderate heat, covered, just until the shells open, discard any that don't open. Remove from heat, and cool until able to handle. Take the whole clams from the shells and save half the shells. Blend together the butter, garlic, parsley, and bread crumbs. Set each clam into a half shell and spread with approximately 1 tsp of the mixture.

Arrange the claims in a shallow baking dish and broil till clams are lightly browned.

Serves 10 — 12

# Stuffed Grape Leaves

## Syria

1 can (1 lb) grape leaves (can be found in gourmet shops)
1 lb ground lamb (use beef if you don't like lamb)
¼ cup uncooked brown rice, washed and drained
1 small can tomato sauce
1/8 tsp allspice
½ cup parsley, finely chopped
1 tbsp virgin olive oil
¼ cup pine nuts, sautéed in olive oil

Make the covering sauce as follows: water enough to cover ¼ the depth of a small baking pan together with 2 tbsp tomato sauce, 1 tbsp olive oil and reserve the juice of 2 lemons.

Rinse each leaf and remove the tough stem and drain them. Mix together the meat, rice, tomato sauce, seasoning, parsley, nuts, and oil. Spread each leaf bottom side up, fill each leaf with a tbsp of the meat mixture, and roll loosely, so the rice can puff without tearing the leaves. Put them close together so they won't come apart. Over all pour the sauce to ¼ the depth of the pan. Cook slowly for 1 hour in a covered pan (low heat, you don't want them to boil, or they will break apart). Check them to make sure there is sufficient sauce, adding more if necessary. After 1 hour, add lemon juice and place in a 325 degree oven uncovered for 45 minutes.

Serve approximately 25

# Stuffed Onions

### Athens

3 large onions
1 lb ground lamb
4 tbsp brown rice (uncooked)
¼ cup parsley, finely chopped
1 tsp freshly ground black pepper
¼ tsp salt
3 tbsp virgin olive oil
3 tbsp lemon juice
½ can tomato sauce (4 – 6 oz)
1 cup water

Meat mixture is made by combining the meat, parsley, spices, 1 – ½ tbsp olive oil, rice, and 1 tbsp lemon juice.

Cut onions in half crossways; place them in boiling water, cook till tender, (approximately 4 – 5 minutes). Discard the water and let the onions cool, then separate layers one by one, forming little cups. Fill each cup with meat mixture. Arrange cups in a baking dish and pour the tomato sauce, water, remaining olive oil and lemon juice mixed together over all. Bake in a pre-heated oven at 375 degrees approximately 45 minutes.

Serves 4 – 6

# Alsatian Vegetable Soup

Alsace borders the Rhine River and Germany

This recipe comes from Strasborg

4 tbsp fresh butter
1 large onion, chopped
1 med shallot, chopped
1 cup celery, chopped
½ lb mushrooms, chopped
1 med potato, peeled and diced
3 med turnips, peeled and diced
5 cups veal stock (see page 3)
¼ tsp crushed marjoram leaves
2 tsp lemon juice
1/3 cup fresh cream
Salt and freshly ground pepper to taste
Chopped chives for garnish

In a 4 quart pan over medium heat, melt butter; add onion, shallot, celery, and mushrooms. Cook until onion is soft. Remove and set aside approximately half the mushrooms. Add potatoes, turnips, veal stock, and marjoram. Bring mixture to a boil; cover, reduce heat and simmer until potatoes and turnips are soft. Puree the mixture and return to pan. Stir in lemon juice, reserved mushrooms and cream. Season to taste with salt and pepper; heat and garnish with chives.

Serves 4 — 6

# Borscht

### Jewish Soul Food

### Russia, Poland, Lithuania, you name it

6 med beets
2 large onions, chopped
3 med cloves garlic, crushed
1 quart veal stock (see page 3)
3 tbsp lemon juice
5 tbsp Vodka, or was it 8 (whichever, tee hee)
6 oz sour cream
1 med bunch chives, chopped

Chop the beets into a deep sauce pan, add onions, veal stock, and season with freshly ground pepper and a pinch of salt. Bring to a boil, cover, reduce heat, and simmer for approximately 45 minutes. Strain and discard the veggies. I don't, but you can if you want to. Add vodka. When this is cool, chill over night, (obviously you prepare this one the day before company is coming). Serve with a heaping tbsp of sour cream, sprinkled with chives. A large chunk of Russian rye would also be nice.

Serves 4—5

# Canh Dua Leo

Vietnamese Cucumber Soup

2 med—large cucumbers
4 chicken breasts, skinned
1 tsp salt
1 tsp freshly ground black pepper
1 tsp MSG
3 tbsp sesame oil
1 tbsp Cilantro, finely chopped
½ med onion, chopped fine

Cut chicken into 2" strips; then place in deep soup kettle, together with 32 oz of water. Bring to a boil and cook chicken until done (approximately 20 minutes). Skim while cooking to keep broth clear. Stir in salt, pepper, and MSG. Add more water if needed. Reduce to a simmer and prepare cucumbers by peeling, then slice lengthwise first, then cross cut them into ½" pieces. Add the cucumbers to the pot and bring to a quick boil for approximately 1 minute.

Ladle into soup bowls, add ¾ tsp sesame oil to each bowl, then garnish with chopped onion and Cilantro and serve.

Serves 4

# Carrot and Parsnip Soup

France

8 tbsp butter
4 cups carrots, coarsely chopped
2 cups parsnips, coarsely chopped
1½ cups green onions, coarsely chopped
(Scallions, Clyde)
1 shallot, coarsely chopped
6 cups chicken stock (see page 1)
1 package herbed croutons (making your own takes
too long)
Pinch of kosher salt
½ tsp freshly ground black pepper
1 cup Crème Faiche
(Whipping cream with a dash of yogurt is a good
substitute)

In a medium saucepan over medium low heat, melt 4 tbsp butter. Add carrots, parsnips, shallot, and green onions; sauté 5 to 6 minutes, stirring constantly. Add chicken stock and bring to a simmer over medium high heat, cover and reduce heat. Simmer until carrots are starting to turn tender. The parsnips will already be very soft. Remove from heat and cool. Transfer ingredients to a blender and puree till smooth. Pour into the sauce pan and reheat; season to taste with the salt and pepper. Garnish with the croutons. Heat the Crème Fraiche, and pass the pitcher of warm crème to top the soup to taste.

Serves 4—6

# Chicken Soup

Also known as Jewish Penicillin

Bobbeh's recipe

1 stewing chicken
Cold water enough to cover the chicken (approx 2 qt)
1 tbsp kosher salt
1 large onion, sliced thin
3 carrots, unpeeled and coarsely chopped
2 stalks celery (leave green tops on), coarsely chopped
3 small parsnips, quartered
1 tbsp Cilantro, finely chopped

Bone the chicken and cut into pieces. Don't forget to leave in the schmaltz, (chicken fat to you uninitiated). Place in a 4—5 quart pan. Add water to about 2" over the chicken. Add salt, onions, carrots, celery, and parsnips. Bring to a boil, skim, and then reduce heat to a simmer. Cover the pot and cook about 1 ½ hours, till chicken is tender, add the cilantro and cook another 30 minutes.

Some recipes call for straining and discarding the veggies, but Bobbeh was never known to waste anything when it came to food, which is to say the old darling never discarded anything, and neither do I.

Serves 4—6

# Corn Chowder

## Eighteenth Century America

I thought since we are going all over the world, we should have some recipes from our own country as well. You will find several spread throughout this book.

1/3 lb salt pork, cubed
(I use thick country bacon and hand slice it myself)
1 large onion, sliced fairly thin
4 med potatoes, diced small
5 cups water
1½ cups milk
2 cups corn cut from the cob (or maybe niblets from the can)
1 tsp salt

Fry the cubed pork in a skillet until crisp. Add onion and cook till onion is golden. Transfer to a 4 qt pan and add water, milk, corn, salt, and diced potatoes. Simmer over a low heat (do not let it boil) for 15—20 minutes; season to taste with freshly ground pepper, and serve. You may wish to float a thick piece of country style bread in the bowl sprinkled with a bit of cheese.

Serves 4

# Crab and Red Pepper Bisque

## All over Spain's Costa del Sol

1½ oz butter
1 tbsp olive oil
1 med onion, peeled and chopped
1 red pepper, seeded and chopped
(Seeds in if you want it hot)
2 stalks celery, rinsed and chopped
1 tsp paprika
2 healthy tbsp Brandy (they have some fine Brandy in Spain)
4 tomatoes, coarsely chopped
10 oz fresh white crabmeat
1½ pints fish stock (see page 2)
½ oz brown rice
Salt and freshly ground black pepper to taste
Healthy squeeze of lemon

Melt the butter with the olive oil in a large frying pan and fry onion, red pepper, and celery over low heat so the veggies soften but do not turn brown. Add paprika and cook for 1 minute, still over low heat, then add the brandy and cook for about 30 seconds to burn off. Stir in tomatoes and add crabmeat reserving 1 tbsp of crabmeat for garnish. Pour in fish stock and add rice. Bring to a bubble, then simmer for 30 minutes or until veggies are soft. Puree smooth in a blender. Place sieve over a clean pan and using the back of a spoon, push as much through the sieve as possible. Discard the debris from inside the sieve. Just before serving, bring bisque back to bubbling, season and add lemon juice. Ladle into warm serving bowls and add reserved crabmeat as a garnish to each.

Serves 4

# Gazpacho

## Mexico

This cold vegetable soup from south of the border only takes approximately 30 to 40 minutes to prepare, but the chilling time is approximately 4 hours, so make it the night before.

1 large cucumber
2 large tomatoes, seeded and chopped very fine
1 large green bell pepper, seeded and chopped very fine
1 small can sliced black olives
¼ cup lime juice
5 cups chicken stock (see page 1)
1 brimming cup tomato juice
1 large clove garlic, minced
½ cup chopped scallions (all except the whiskers)
1 tbsp chopped thyme
Tabasco for seasoning (to taste)

Peel cucumber and cut in half lengthwise; scrape out and discard the seeds. Chop the cucumber very fine. In a large mixing bowl combine cucumber, tomatoes, bell pepper, olives, lime juice, chicken stock, tomato juice, garlic, scallions, and thyme; season to taste with the Tabasco. Cover and refrigerate for at least 4 hours.

Serves 6 — 8

# Leek Soup

France

20 oz chicken stock (see page 1)
5 cups sliced leeks (medium thin, white part only)
3 cups potatoes, peeled and diced small
1 cup Crème Fraiche
(Whipping cream with a dash of yogurt is a good substitute)
4 tbsp dry vermouth (or is it 5?)
I always seem to err on the side of more is better
A healthy pinch of salt
Chopped chives for garnish

In a 4 quart pan combine the chicken stock, leeks, and potatoes. Bring to a boil; cover and reduce heat to a simmer until the veggies are soft (approximately 15—20 minutes).

Puree the mixture in a blender then return to pan. Stir in the Crème and Vermouth. Season to taste with salt and freshly ground pepper. Garnish with chopped chives.

Serve it hot and it is called Potage Parmentier, serve it cold and you may recognize it by it's other name: VICHYSSOISE.

Serves 6

Bon Apetit

# Lentil and Bulgar Soup

Bobbeh's recipe

2 cups lentils
5 cups chicken stock (see page 1)
2 cups hot water
1 cup medium coarse Bulgar
1 tsp kosher salt
2 med onions, cut in half then thin sliced
4 tbsp olive oil
1 tsp ground cumin
½ tbsp red pepper flakes

Bring the chicken stock to a boil, add the lentils, lower the heat, cover and simmer for approximately 20 minutes. Mix the Bulgar and hot water in a bowl and allow the grain to absorb the water. Add the Bulgar to the lentils, and salt. Stir to mix well and cover. Sauté the onions over a medium heat in the olive oil, stirring all the while till onions are soft and caramel colored. Add cumin about half the way through this process. Stir the pepper flakes into the onions; then stir the onions into the lentils. This makes a thick hearty soup that will warm your cockles (what the hell ever they are), and it's spicy too. Serve with a large chunk of Russian rye or black bread.

Serves 4 — 6

# Minestrone

Italy, a la Genovese

4 quarts water
1 lb ham chunks
1 lb bony chicken parts
½ lb sliced bacon (chop it up a little)
3 cups diced potatoes
2 cups diced celery
3 med zucchini, sliced in ½" pieces
2 cups sliced leeks
1 lb green beans, cut in 2" lengths
½ cup ditalini (salad style macaroni), or
tripolini
¾ lb shelled peas
3 cups shredded white cabbage
2 tsp salt
Pesto sauce (see page 14)

Combine water, ham, chicken, and bacon; bring to a boil, cover and reduce to a simmer for 2 hours. Strain, and reserve stock, discarding the meat and bones. Bring stock to a boil, add potatoes, cover and simmer 12−15 minutes. Add celery, zucchini, leeks, green beans, and pasta and simmer an additional 10 minutes. Stir in peas and cabbage; cook for an additional 10 minutes; salt to taste. Ladle soup into bowls and spoon in Pesto sauce to taste.

Serves approximately 10

# Mulligatawny

This curry flavored soup dates to the fur trade era

Most trading posts of any size in North America had curry powders by 1830.

1 stewing chicken, cut into pieces
½ cup of lard
1 large yellow onion
1 green pepper, seeded and diced
3 stalks celery, diced
3 apples, cored and diced
1 tbsp curry powder
1 tbsp flour
1 qt chicken stock (see page 1)
4 cups white rice (I prefer brown rice—more flavor)

Dust the chicken with flour, salt and pepper; brown in hot lard. Remove chicken, and fry vegetables and apples in the hot lard until tender. Add curry powder and stir well. Add chicken and stock and simmer till tender, (approximately 2 hours). Remove chicken, de-bone and chop the meat. Return to the kettle, add rice and cook till rice is tender.

Serves 4—6

# Onion Soup

France, Soupe A l'Oignon

This one is famous all over the world (with good reason)

1 tbsp olive oil
6 tbsp butter
8 med onions, sliced thin
8 cups veal stock (see page 3)
¼ cup port wine
1 cup shredded parmesan cheese

Heat oil and 3 tbsp butter in a 4 quart pan over medium heat. Add onions and cook stirring until soft and caramel colored, but not brown, (approximately 30 minutes). Add veal stock and bring to a boil, cover, reduce heat and simmer for approximately 30 minutes. Season to your taste with salt and freshly ground pepper, then stir in the port wine. Pour into earthenware bowls (ovenproof you know). Float a large chunk of toasted French bread in each bowl and sprinkle with the parmesan cheese. Melt the remaining butter and mist it over the floating bread, then bake in a 400 degree oven for approximately 10 minutes, then turn on broiler to lightly toast the cheese. Don't just stand there Clyde, eat.

Serves 6 — 8

# Shrimp and Watercress Soup

## Vietnam

3 cups chicken stock (see page 1)
4 green onions, very thinly sliced
1 tbsp Nuoc Mam (see page 13)
½ lb small to med shrimp, peeled and de-veined
1 med bunch of watercress, chopped
Salt and freshly ground pepper, to taste

Bring stock to a boil; reduce to a simmer. Add green onions and Nuoc Mam; season with salt and pepper.

Add shrimp to soup and simmer until opaque white. Add watercress and simmer until just wilted, and serve.

Serves 4

# Stracciatella

Rome, Italy

4 cups chicken stock (see page 1)
½ cup water
¼ cup tripolini
3 tbsp grated Parmesan cheese
1 tbsp chopped parsley
1 well beaten egg
A healthy dash of ground nutmeg

In a medium saucepan, bring chicken stock and water to a boil. Add tripolini and cook uncovered, just until pasta becomes tender. Reduce heat and stir in Parmesan, parsley, and nutmeg. Slowly pour beaten egg into simmering broth. Swirl once very gently. Serve immediately.

This is somewhat similar to Chinese egg drop soup

Serves 4—6

# Tomato Soup with Fresh Basil

This is found all over the Cote d'Azur region of France

3 tbsp fresh butter
1 large onion, sliced
5 large tomatoes, peeled, seeded, and chopped
(4—5 cups)
¼ cup of fresh basil leaves
½ tsp salt
½ tsp sugar
¼ tsp freshly ground pepper
16 oz chicken stock (see page 1)
1 tbsp pastina (any tiny soup pasta will do)

In a 4 qt pan over medium heat, melt butter, add onion and cook till onion is limp. Stir in tomatoes, basil, salt, sugar, and pepper. Bring to a boil over high heat, stirring constantly. Cover, reduce heat and simmer for approximately 10 minutes. Puree mixture and set aside. In a small pan over high heat, bring chicken stock to a boil, add pasta, and reduce heat to medium, and cook until pasta is tender (approx 8 minutes). Stir tomato puree into stock and heat to a simmer. Serve immediately.

Serves 4—6

# Chicken Cacciatore

Italy, were else Clyde

3 medium onions, sliced
3 med cloves garlic, well minced
3 tbsp olive oil
1 3lb frying chicken, cut up
1 16 oz can tomatoes, un-drained and cut up
1 8 oz can tomato sauce
1 large green pepper, seeded and cut into ½ inch pieces
1 3 oz can mushroom stems and pieces, drained
2 bay leaves
2 tsp oregano
1 tsp salt
¼ tsp freshly ground pepper
½ cup dry white wine

In a large skillet, cook unions and garlic in olive oil over medium heat, till onions are tender. Remove onions and set aside. Add a little more oil in the skillet and brown the chicken pieces over medium heat for approximately 10 – 12 minutes turning to brown evenly. Return onions to skillet. Combine un-drained tomatoes, tomato sauce, mushrooms, green peppers, bay leaves, oregano, 1 tsp salt and ¼ tsp freshly ground black pepper, and pour over chicken in skillet. Cover and simmer about 25 – 30 minutes. Stir in the wine. Cook uncovered over a low heat approximately 15 minutes more, or until chicken is tender (turn occasionally). Discard the bay leaves and transfer the chicken to a bed of Risotto, (see page 70). Spoon the sauce over all and dig in.
     Serves 4

# Roast Chicken and Parsley

## Italy

This is a popular dish in Perugia, a city in the Umbria region.

1 3—4 pound roasting chicken
Salt and pepper to taste
½ cup olive oil
¼ cup lemon juice
1 full tsp ground thyme
1 large bunch parsley

Wash and dry the bird, salt and pepper it inside and out. Blend the olive oil, lemon juice and thyme. Rub this mixture all over the bird inside and out. Stuff the bird loosely with the parsley and bake uncovered in a 325 degree oven for approximately 1 ½ hours.

Serves 3—4

# Cholent

Bobbeh's recipe

This one is a 24 hour recipe. It was made the day before so as to be eaten as the afternoon meal on Shabbas (Sabbath)

4 lbs beef brisket, cut up in chunks
5 tbsp olive oil
4 onions, chopped well
4 large cloves garlic, crushed
1 medium can lima beans
Bobbeh used dried beans (canned is quicker and easier)
1 medium can chick peas (Garabonzo beans)
4 stalks celery, chopped
4 carrots, chopped
4 potatoes, chopped
½ tbsp salt (to taste)
½ tsp freshly ground pepper
¼ tsp ginger
2 cups veal stock (see page 3)

Heat olive oil in a Dutch oven, add onion, brown them then add the meat and brown it well; season with the salt, pepper, and crushed garlic. Drain and reserve the liquid from the lima beans and chick peas. Add beans, peas, celery, carrots, potatoes, and ginger; toss to combine. Add the liquid from the beans and peas together with the veal stock. The liquid should cover the contents. Put the lid on and cook at 225 degrees for 24 hours. Add a little liquid if needed. GOOD SHABBAS!
Serves 6 — 8

# Couscous

### Israel, and almost all of North Africa

¾ cup olive oil
2 lbs lamb stewing meat, cubed
2 lbs boned chicken breasts, cubed
4 large onions, chopped
4 tomatoes, cubed
1 green pepper, chopped
1 tsp freshly ground black pepper
2 tsp tumeric
2 tsp salt
12 oz sweet peas
10 oz artichoke hearts
1 large can chick peas (Garabanzo beans)
5 cups water
1 8 — 10 oz. Package Bulgar (cracked wheat)

Heat oil in a Dutch oven, or other deep pot. Add lamb, chicken, and onion; cook until lamb and chicken are well browned. Add tomatoes, blend together and cook over low heat for 10 — 12 minutes. Add green pepper, tumeric, black pepper, salt, and water; stir together. Cover and simmer for 1 hour. Add peas, garabanzos with their liquid, and the artichokes and simmer an additional 20 minutes. Cook Bulgar as directed on the package. Put Bulgar in a large serving bowl. Pour the meat mixture over the Bulgar and let stand approximately 10 minutes to allow the Bulgar to absorb the juices.

Serves 10 — 12

# Crab and Fish Cakes

## Thailand

12 oz orange roughy fillet
¼ pt of fish stock (see page 2)
10 oz fresh white crabmeat
10 oz peeled, diced potatoes
½ oz unsalted butter
Salt and freshly ground black pepper (to taste)
Grated zest of 1 med lemon
Healthy dash of green Tabasco sauce
1 tbsp coarsely chopped coriander
6 tbsp sunflower oil
3 heads of bok choy, quartered
4 tbsp oyster sauce (obtained from Asian deli)
2 tbsp Chinese rice wine (obtained from Asian deli)
Healthy dash of spicy oriental fish sauce (see pg 13)

Poach fish in fish stock. Drain. Remove skin and flake flesh into a bowl. Add flaked crabmeat. Cook diced potatoes till softened. Drain and crush with a potato masher, adding the butter; season. Add to fish and crabmeat with lemon zest and Tabasco; season to taste. Add coriander. On a floured board, shape mix into 4 cakes. Chill for approximately 30 minutes. Shallow—fry cakes in 2 tbsp hot sunflower oil until golden on both sides and heated through. At the same time, heat the remaining oil in a wok and add the bok choy. Stir fry for 1 minute; then add oyster sauce, rice wine and fish sauce. Stir fry for 1 additional minute then arrange on plates and perch the cakes on top.
Serves 4

# Haggis

Scotland, Lassie, Scotland

1 cleaned and well rinsed Sheep's stomach bag
(Scotland the brave lassie; read on)
1 lb suet (remember these people like bagpipes too)
1 lb sheep's liver, boiled and finely diced
1 sheep's heart, boiled and finely diced
1 pair of sheep's lungs, boiled and finely diced
2 sheep's kidneys boiled twice, and finely diced
2 lbs dry oats (oatmeal to you, Clyde)
1 large onion, chopped
1 tsp salt
2 tsp freshly ground black pepper
2 large cups brown ale

Toast the oatmeal in a dry skillet until it is crisp. Mix all
the ingredients except the stomach together, and moisten with
one cup of water and one cup of ale. Fill the stomach bag just
over half full, then press out the air and sew up the bag leaving
a bit of room for expansion. Prick the bag in several places with
an ice pick or it will burst. Place in a large stock pot of boiling
water and boil it for for 4 hours. That second cup of ale? Drink
it, you twit!

The only socially redeeming value I have been able to find
in a Haggis is that traditionally, it is to be washed down with
copious quantities of Scotch Whiskey (Single Malt preferably).

Serves 4 — 6 if you really care

UP THE REBELS!!!

# Lamb Cutlets on Fresh Asparagus

Alencon in Normandy

6 oz baby leeks, trimmed
1 tbsp virgin olive oil
6 small lamb cutlets
Salt and freshly ground black pepper (to taste)
½ wineglass red wine (Merlot is my personal choice)
¼ pt of vegetable stock (see pg 4)
1½ oz unsalted butter
1 tbsp fresh mint leaves, shredded
3 oz fresh asparagus tips

Blanch leeks in lightly salted water for 2 minutes. Drain, blot dry and reserve. Heat oil in a frying pan and cook cutlets until brown on both sides but still pink in the middle. Season and remove from pan, keeping them warm. Pour wine into pan and stir to scrape loose any sediment. Add stock and bring to bubbling. Reduce heat slightly, then add ½ oz of butter, season and stir in shredded mint. At the same time, melt remaining butter in a wok or large frying pan. Over a medium heat stir fry reserved leeks and asparagus tips for approximately 2 minutes or until just becoming tender. Season and spoon leeks onto warmed serving plates; perch cutlets on top. Spoon mint gravy over and serve immediately.

Serves 3—4

# Liver Napoli

## Italy

I found this one in Naples, and not being a great fan of liver, I was pleasantly surprised.

½ cup breadcrumbs
3 tbsp grated Parmesan cheese
½ tsp garlic powder
¼ tsp crushed oregano leaves (or powdered if you prefer)
1 lb calf liver, sliced ½ inch thick and trimmed
of membrane
Salt and pepper to season
1 large egg, beaten
3 tbsp butter
3 tbsp olive oil
5 — 6 oz mozzarella cheese, sliced
8 — 10 oz tomato sauce (see page 6)

In a shallow pan, combine breadcrumbs, garlic powder, parmesan cheese, and oregano. Sprinkle each slice of meat with a little salt and pepper, dip into the beaten egg, then in the breadcrumbs. Heat the butter and oil in a frying pan until it is very hot. Fry the liver pieces until browned on both sides, about 3—4 minutes. Drain meat on paper towels then layer the meat with the mozzarella slices in 10 inch square baking dish. Pour tomato sauce over the liver and cheese. Bake at 350 degrees for about 15 minutes.

Serves 4

# Moussaka

### Greece

Got this from the Fireside Restaurant in Glifada, a suburb of Athens.

1 medium eggplant
Olive oil for frying
1 lb ground lamb (use veal if you don't like lamb)
1 medium onion, chopped fine
1 large egg
3 bay leaves
½ tsp sugar
8 — 10 oz tomato sauce (see page 6)
Salt and pepper to taste

Peel and slice eggplant (1/4 inch slices) and fry in olive oil until golden on both sides. Line an un-greased baking pan (9 x 12) with approximately half of the eggplant slices. Mix all the ingredients together; spread over the eggplant and top with the remaining slices. Put the bay leaves on top; bake uncovered in a 350 degree oven for approximately 1 hour.

Serves 4 — 6

# Osso buco

## A la Milanese

2 — 3 lbs veal shanks cut into 2 — 3 inch pieces
4 tbsp all purpose flour
6 tbsp olive oil
1 cup chopped onion
¼ cup chopped carrots
¼ cup chopped celery
2 cloves garlic, well minced
1 large can (28 oz) tomatoes, chopped
1½ cup dry white wine
1 bay leaf
3 tsp grated orange peel
1/3 cup veal stock (see page 3)
½ tsp crushed coriander

Sprinke the meat well with salt and freshly ground black pepper. Coat the meat lightly with flour. In a Dutch oven, brown the meat slowly in the hot olive oil; remove the meat. Add onion, carrot, celery, and garlic; cook till onion and celery are tender. Return meat to Dutch oven. Stir in un-drained tomatoes, wine, bay leaf, orange peel, veal stock, coriander, 1 cup water, ½ tsp salt and a healthy dash of freshly ground pepper. Bring to a boil; reduce heat. Cover and simmer for 1 — 1 ½ hours or until meat is tender. Remove the meat to a warming tray. Boil broth mixture very gently uncovered for about 15 to 20 minutes or until desired thickness. Arrange the meat on a Milanese style Risotto (see page 70). Spoon the broth over the meat and serve.
Serves 4 — 6

# Paella

## Spain

4 chicken breasts, boned, skinned, and cut into strips
10 — 12 oz chorizo, well crumbled
1 large yellow onion, well chopped
1 clove garlic, minced
1 tsp paprika
3 tbsp fresh parsley, well chopped
¼ - ½ tsp freshly ground black pepper
1 cup chicken stock (see page 1)
1 cup rice, uncooked (I prefer brown rice, suit yourself)
2½ tbsp pimento, chopped
16 oz (2 medium cans) artichoke hearts, drained
½ - ¾ lb large shrimp cooked and de-veined
(Tiger Prawns work well)
1 cup fresh green peas
½ tsp saffron (this is optional since it is quite expensive)
2 tbsp olive oil

Cut chicken in strips and brown in the olive oil; add the chorizo and heat well. Remove the chicken and chorizo from pan and sauté onion and garlic until just brown. Add paprika, pepper, parsley and chicken stock; bring to a boil. Add rice and pimento. Cover and simmer approximately 45 — 50 minutes or until the rice is cooked. Add the chicken, chorizo, artichokes, shrimp, and sprinkle the peas over the top, then sprinkle the saffron over it all. Cover and simmer an additional 10 — 12 minutes until all is heated clear through.

Serves 4 — 6

# Pork Chops with Corn and Pimento

## Southern Style

I found this one at a truck stop in Dothan, Alabama.

8 pork loin chops, country cut, (that means thick, Clyde)
¼ cup green peppers, seeded and finely chopped
½ cup onions, finely chopped
1½ tbsp butter
1 large egg, beaten
1½ cups herbed bread crumbs
¾ cup corn niblets
4 tbsp pimento, finely chopped
½ tsp salt
¼ tsp freshly ground black pepper

In a small saucepan, cook green pepper and onion in butter till tender. Combine egg, breadcrumbs, corn, pimento, salt and pepper. Pour the onion and pepper into the breadcrumb mixture and stir well. Cut a pocket in each chop almost to the bone. Season the cavity with a little salt and pepper. Spoon approximately ¼ cup of the mixture into each chop and secure with a toothpick. Bake in a 325 degree oven approximately 12—15 minutes, then turn and bake an additional 10 minutes or until done.

Serves 8

# Pot Roast

### Hungarian style ala Budapest

5 to 6 pound pot roast, larded with ¼ inch strips of
salt pork
5 tbsp olive oil
1 tsp kosher salt
3 heaping tsp paprika, divided
½ tsp nutmeg
¾ cup veal stock (see page 3)
1 cup sour cream

Sear the pot roast well in the olive oil. Place in a Dutch oven
with salt and 1 ½ tsp paprika, nutmeg and veal stock. Cover and
cook 30 minutes to the pound at 300 degrees, adding additional
liquid if needed. When it is done, skim excess fat from the
liquid. Blend remaining paprika and sour cream and add. Don't
just stand there, it is time to eat this wonderful creation.

Serves 6 — 8

# Rabbit in a Pickled Onion Sauce

## Italy

2 — 3 pound frying rabbit, cut into pieces
Salt, pepper, and nutmeg to taste
¼ cup fresh butter
1 medium to large onion, chopped fine
1 clove of garlic, minced
1 8 oz can of Tomato sauce
1/3 cup sweet vermouth
1 bay leaf
¼ tsp black peppercorns
¼ cup drained small white pickled onions
½ cup of whipping cream

Sprinkle the rabbit pieces with salt, pepper, and nutmeg. Melt butter in a large deep frying pan over medium heat. Add rabbit a few pieces at a time and brown well, remove when browned. To the same pan add chopped onion and cook stirring till soft. Mix in garlic, tomato sauce, vermouth, bay leaf and peppercorns; then add rabbit and pickled onions. Bring to a boil, cover, reduce heat and simmer until rabbit is tender (approximately 60 minutes). Remove to a warm serving dish; keep warm. Skim fat from your cooking liquid. Add cream and bring to a boil over high heat; continue to cook until sauce thickens slightly. Pour sauce over rabbit and dig in.

Serves 4 — 6

# Rabbit in White Wine

### France

You can substitute chicken if you're not crazy about eating Bugs Bunny.

1 fryer rabbit, (approx 3 lbs) cut into pieces
Salt and freshly ground black pepper (to taste)
¼ cup virgin olive oil
1 lb small mushrooms
3 tbsp flour
1¾ cup dry white wine
10 small onions, (yellow, approx 1" diameter) peeled
½ cup chopped parsley
½ tsp dry rosemary
2 cloves garlic, minced
4 tbsp butter
2½ cups herbed croutons

Sprinkle meat with salt; heat oil in large frying pan (medium low heat). Add the meat and cook till browned on all sides, then reserve. Add mushrooms to pan, cook over medium heat till they are lightly browned. Remove the pan from the fire and stir in the flour, wine, onions, parsley, rosemary, and garlic. Return meat to pan, bring to a boil, cover and simmer until meat is tender, (approx 40 –45 minutes). Arrange the meat in serving dish surrounded by croutons and sprinkled with springs of rosemary.

Serves 4

# Risotto

## Milano

¼ cup onion finely chopped
½ cup prosciutto, finely chopped
3 tbsp butter
3 cups veal stock (see page 3)
1 cup long grain rice
½ tsp salt
Healthy dash freshly ground black pepper

In a medium saucepan, cook onion and prosciutto in butter till onion becomes tender. Stir in veal stock, rice, salt and pepper, bring to a rolling boil; reduce heat to low. Cover with a tight fitting lid. Continue cooking for approximately 15 minutes. Do not lift lid. Remove from heat and let stand 5 — 6 minutes. Rice should now be tender and the broth mixture creamy.

Serves 6

# Roast Pork with Herbs

France

This one comes from Dijon in eastern central France.

3 lb boned pork loin roast (rolled and tied)
¾ tsp thyme
½ tsp powdered sage
Salt, and freshly ground black pepper (to taste)
2 med onions, finely chopped
2 cups chicken stock (see page 1)
¼ cup Madeira
1 tbsp cornstarch
2 tbsp water

Place meat in medium roasting pan. Rub thyme, sage, salt, and pepper on meat. Ring meat with onions and add ½ cup of chicken stock. Bake uncovered at 325 degrees for approximately 2 hours. After 1 hour, pour the remaining 1 ½ cups of chicken stock into pan; baste the meat a couple of times during the last hour. When the meat is done remove from oven. In a small frying pan over a medium heat, warm the Madeira; set it aflame and shake the pan until flame goes out. Pour over the meat; then transfer meat to a serving dish. Place roasting pan on high heat, and stir as the juice begins to boil. Combine cornstarch and water; add small amounts at a time, stirring continuously, until sauce is at the desired thickness. Pour into a gravy boat and pass at the table to be spooned over sliced meat.

Serves 4 — 6

# Sauerbraten

## Germany

2 lbs beef rump roast
1 large onion, peeled and cut into rings
6 peppercorns
3 cloves
1 bay leaf
½ pint of vinegar
¾ pint of water
This one needs to be started way ahead of time.

Place meat in a large earthenware bowl with the water, vinegar, spices, and onion rings. Make sure the meat is completely covered by the liquid. Cover and marinate in a cool place (refrigerator) for 4—6 days. Remove the meat from the marinade and dry with a cloth before cooking.

2 oz fat for cooking
1 pint water
1 thick slice gingerbread
2 tsp cornstarch
1 tbsp cold water

Melt the fat in a skillet, put the meat in and brown it very quickly on all sides. Add a pinch of salt. Pour in about half a pint of hot water, add the gingerbread and let simmer gently covered, adding a little water as necessary. When it is cooked, serve it with the gravy that it has been cooked in, thickened with the cornstarch that you have blended with the last tbsp of water.

Serves 4

# Sole with Grapes

France

1½ lb sole fillets
1 cup seedless green grapes
3 tbsp fresh butter
½ cup whipping cream
Ground nutmeg (to taste)
Salt (to taste)

Sprinkle fish lightly with salt and nutmeg, dust with flour, shake off excess.

In large frying pan over medium heat, melt 2 tbsp butter, add fish and cook turning once, until fish is golden brown on both sides, and flakes easily when pierced with a fork, (approximately 5 – 6 minutes). Transfer to a serving dish and keep warm.

Add grapes to pan with the rest of the butter, and swirl over a high heat only until warm and a bright green. Pour over fish.

Stir cream into pan and boil over high heat, stirring until it turns a golden color. Drizzle sauce over fish and serve immediately.

Serves 4

# Steak with Green Peppercorns

### France

2 lbs boneless beef steak (tenderize with a meat mallet)
2 tbsp fresh butter
1 tbsp virgin olive oil
6 — 7 tbsp brandy (try 8, I did)
½ cup shallots, minced
2 tbsp canned green peppercorns (don't rinse)
¾ cup crème fraiche
(Whipping cream with a dash of yogurt is a good substitute)
1½ tbsp Dijon mustard
½ tsp dry tarragon

Salt to taste, sauté steak in butter and olive oil. When meat is cooked, add brandy and set aflame, shake the pan till flame dies. Remove meat to a warming pan.

Add shallots to pan, cook over high heat stirring till soft (approximately 3 — 4 minutes). Add peppercorns to pan along with crème fraiche, mustard, and tarragon, stirring with meat juices. Boil over high heat stirring till shiny bubbles appear, (approximately 4 minutes). Season the meat with salt and freshly ground pepper (to taste) and spoon sauce over meat, then eat you twit.

Serves 4

# Stuffed Peppers

### New Orleans Style

6 large green peppers
½ lb ground pork
1 cup precooked shrimp, (peeled and de-clawed) chopped fine
1 large onion, chopped fine
½ cup celery, chopped fine
2 cloves garlic, minced
3 cups herbed bread crumbs
1 large tomato, peeled and chopped
½ tsp salt
¼ tsp freshly ground black pepper
1 tbsp Tabasco

Cut tops off peppers, remove seeds and membrane and discard. Cook peppers in boiling water for approximately 5 minutes. Invert and drain peppers, turn right side up and sprinkle insides lightly with salt. Cook pork, onion, celery, and garlic till pork is well—browned and onion is tender. Stir in chopped shrimp and cook another 3 minutes. Stir bread crumbs, tomato, salt, pepper, and hot sauce into pork mixture. Stuff peppers.

Place peppers in a 9 x 12 baking dish. Bake uncovered at 350 degrees for approximately 30 minutes.

Serves 6

# Stuffed Pork Roast

## Louisiana

In this part of the south, nothing seems to go better with mashed potatoes and gravy than a nice pork roast for Sunday dinner. This is one of those longer than 2 hour recipes I spoke about back at the beginning of the book. There are a few (but not many).

3 ½ - 4 lb boneless pork loin roast
¼ cup onion, chopped very fine
¼ cup green pepper, seeded, cored and chopped very fine
3 cloves garlic, minced
½ tsp salt
½ tsp freshly ground black pepper
½ tsp red pepper flakes

Combine all the ingredients (except the meat Clyde) in a mixing bowl and mix well. Cut 12—15 deep slits in the meat, approximately 1" wide at random. Stuff these slits with some of the stuffing mixture. Place the roast fat side up, on a rack in a roasting pan. Rub the remaining mixture all over the meat. Roast uncovered at 325 degrees for approximately 3 hours.

Serves 6 — 8

# Wiener Schnitzel

### Germany

4 veal scallops
1 tbsp flour
1 large egg
2 oz herbed breadcrumbs
4 tbsp cooking oil
½ pint water
3 — 4 tbsp sour cream
Salt and freshly ground black pepper (to taste)

Season the meat; dip in flour, then in the beaten egg, then in the breadcrumbs. Fry in the hot oil on both sides until brown. Remove; add water and sour cream to the oil. Stir until well blended, then pour over the meat.

Serve garnished with lemon slices and capers. You may also add a few anchovies to the garnish if you like, but personally, NOT ON YOUR LIFE.

You can serve just about anything for side dishes as this goes well with almost anything.

Serves 4

# Bananas Foster

### New Orleans Style

4 small ripe bananas
¼ cup lemon juice
2/3 cup brown sugar (packed)
1/3 cup fresh butter
2 tbsp banana liqueur
3 tbsp spiced rum (or was it 4 ?)
Dash of ground cinnamon
½ qt French vanilla ice cream

Peel bananas and cut in half lengthwise, then crosswise. Brush with a bit of lemon juice to prevent them from darkening. In a skillet, heat brown sugar and butter over a medium heat till melted stirring occasionally. Add bananas to the mixture and cook uncovered for 3—4 minutes, turning once. Sprinkle with cinnamon, and drizzle the banana liqueur over all.

In a small saucepan heat the spiced rum till just warm. Ignite and pour the rum over the lot. Serve over vanilla ice cream.

Serves 4

# Clafloutis Limousin

### France

Northeast of Bordeaux, is the region known as Limousin, which is where this delightful baked cherry pudding comes from.

3 cups pitted cherries
3 cups of cherry brandy
Grated zest of 1 lemon
½ cup sugar
1 full cup whipping cream
4 eggs
2 tbsp vanilla extract
½ tsp fresh ground nutmeg
1 cup flour

Preheat oven to 350 degrees. In a small bowl combine cherries and brandy and let marinate for 30 minutes or so. In a food processor, blend lemon zest and sugar, blending until you can no longer see bits of yellow. Add cream, eggs, vanilla extract, and nutmeg, and process approximately 10 seconds. Add flour and give it a quick swirl to blend. Grease a 9" diameter baking pan with butter. Drain the cherries, (save the brandy you fool) and pour into pan. Pour batter over top. Bake until well browned and risen, (approximately 30 minutes). Transfer to a wire rack and cool for approximately 10 – 15 minutes. Cut into squares and serve with French Vanilla ice cream.

Serves 6

# Crema de Mango

## Mexico

Mango Cream is a wonderful Mexican dessert, which goes especially well after a spicy meal, (it is quite cooling).

6 large ripe mangoes
Sugar (to taste)
2 large oranges, peeled, seeded, and cut into small pieces
1 tbsp lemon juice
2 ½ cups whipping cream
¾ cup chopped pecans

Peel and pit mangoes. In a blender, whirl fruit until pureed. Transfer to a bowl and season to taste with the sugar. Stir in orange pieces and lemon juice. Whip the cream and fold into the mango mixture. Pour into parfait glasses and sprinkle with the chopped pecans.

Serves 10

# Croissants aux Pignons

### Pine Nut Crescents

You will find this delicious cookie all over the Provence region in France. They go well with coffee after a light meal.

½ lb fresh butter (softened)
2/3 cup brown sugar (firmly packed)
3 egg yokes
1 tsp grated orange peel
¾ tsp vanilla extract
2 1/3 cups flour
½ cup pine nuts
3 tbsp honey

Beat together butter and sugar until creamy. Add egg yokes, one at a time, beating well after each one, so as to blend thoroughly. Stir in orange peel, vanilla extract, and flour. For each cookie, roll approximately 2 tsp of dough with your palms into a rope approximately 2 ½ - 3 inches long. On a greased baking sheet, shape each rope into a crescent, leaving about 2 inches between each cookie. Press pine nuts onto surfaces of the cookies. In a small pan over low heat, warm the honey, stirring till it becomes liquid. Brush honey gently over cookies, taking care to get as little as possible on the pan as it will scorch. Bake in a 325 degree oven for 20 minutes or until golden. Immediately transfer cookies to a wire rack to cool, then serve.

Makes approximately 3 dozen

# German Coffee Cake

Darmstadt, Germany

3 cups flour
4 tsp baking powder
1 tsp salt
¼ tsp nutmeg
¼ tsp cinnamon
¾ cup sugar
¼ cup vegetable shortening (Crisco works well)
2 eggs
1 cup milk

Sift together flour, baking powder, salt, spices, and sugar. Work the dry ingredients into the shortening. Add eggs and milk, stir till smooth. Pour into a greased 9 x 12 pan.

Topping

¼ cup vegetable shortening
1 cup brown sugar
1/8 tsp salt
¼ cup flour
½ tsp cinnamon
1 cup coarsely chopped black walnuts

With a fork blend all but the walnuts, then spread evenly on top of the batter in the pan, then sprinkle with walnuts. Bake in a 350 degree oven for 30 minutes.

# Poached Pears in Red Wine

### Rome

6 large firm Bartlett pears
2 cups dry red wine
1 cup sugar
¼ tsp anise seed
2 whole sticks cinnamon
3 unpeeled lemon slices

In a saucepan large enough to accommodate 6 pears standing side by side, combine the wine, sugar, anise seed, cinnamon sticks, and lemon slices. Bring to a boil, stirring lightly till sugar is dissolved. Remove cores from the blossom end of the pears leaving the stem end intact. Set the fruit into the boiling syrup and boil covered for approximately 10 minutes, turning occasionally so that all portions of the fruit are at times submerged in the syrup. When the fruit is heated through thoroughly, but still retains its shape, lift from the syrup with a slotted spoon and transfer to a serving dish.

Boil syrup at a high heat, uncovered until reduced to approximately 1 cup. Pour over pears. Serve warm with the pears standing stem up (attencione).

Serves 6

# Russian Style Apple Pudding

Bobbeh's recipe

1 large loaf stale Russian rye bread, crumbed
¾ cup fresh butter
Peel from half a lemon grated
Peel of one medium orange grated
1/3 cup dry sherry
½ cup sugar
4 large apples, cored, peeled, and thinly sliced
3 cups sour cream

Sauté crumbs in butter, add grated lemon peel, grated orange peel, sherry, and sugar. Make a layer of crumb mixture in bottom of a buttered baking dish. Add a layer of apple slices, sprinkle with additional sugar, alternate layers of crumbs and apples until dish is full, ending with a layer of crumbs on top. Dot with butter and bake in a pre heated oven at 325 degrees for 45 minutes. Serve with a dollop of sour cream.

Serves 6

# Tishpishti

### Honey Syruped Cake

This one comes from Turkey, I found it in Istanbul, as well as Incirlik, and Izmir. This is a dessert at Passover time.

4 ½ cups matzo meal
1 ½ cups sugar
1 ½ cups olive oil
1 tsp crushed cloves
1 tsp cinnamon
¾ cup water
1 cup coarsely chopped black walnuts
2 eggs
Whole almonds for topping (shelled of course)

Combine all ingredients except almonds and mix until well blended (use your hands—they work best). Put mixture into a 9 x 12 pan. Score the batter with a knife into squares. Press an almond into the top of each square. Bake at 375 degrees for approximately 45 minutes or until golden. Allow to cool, then re-cut the scoring completely through and allow to cool completely.

1½ cup sugar
3 tbsp honey
1 tsp lemon juice
½ cup water
In a saucepan, boil all ingredients; cook till syrup becomes thick. Pour over the Tishpishti and let stand for several hours.
Serves 25

# Sweet Potato Molasses Pie

## Louisiana

3 med sweet potatoes
½ cup brown sugar, packed
3 tbsp molasses
1 tsp ground cinnamon
½ tsp ground ginger
½ tsp ground nutmeg
¼ tsp salt
3 slightly beaten eggs
¼ cup milk
Pastry dough to line 9" pie plate (any single crust
recipe is ok)

In medium saucepan cook raw sweet potatoes in salted boiling water for 20—25 minutes or until tender. Drain, cool slightly and peel. Mash cooled sweet potatoes. In a large mixing bowl combine mashed sweet potatoes, brown sugar, molasses, cinnamon, ginger, nutmeg and salt. Add eggs and milk to the mixture, and mix well. Pour the sweet potato mixture into the previously prepared pie shell and place in a 375 degree oven for approximately 20 minutes, covering the edge of the pie with foil. Remove the foil and bake for another 30 minutes, or till a knife inserted about halfway between the center and the edge comes out clean. Cool on a wire rack. Cover and chill. Serve with a dollop of whipped cream if you like.

Serves 8

# Extra recipes and notes

# Extra recipes and notes

# Extra recipes and notes